OUT FROM UNDER THE BUSHEL

How to Share Your Faith With Confidence

OUT FROM UNDER THE BUSHEL

How to Share Your Faith With Confidence

by John Ott

The Wesley Press
Indianapolis, Indiana

Published by The Wesley Press, Indianapolis, Indiana 46250-0434

International Standard Book Number: 0-89827-046-4

WHAT IS EVANGELISM?

Evangelism is one of the most misunderstood, misused, and ignored areas of the church today. It is one of the greatest sources of frustration, guilt, and fear for laymen and pastors alike.

What is this thing Christ left for us to do before He went to His Father? Why does it leave us feeling like guilt-ridden failures every time we hear a sermon telling us to go? Why was evangelism so dynamic in the early church, yet seems so absent in my church today? What is evangelism and why should you do it?

I have found three basic misconceptions about what evangelism is. These are so prevailing that they must be addressed right here at the outset of this book.

Misconception #1. Evangelism is the active, personal effort of Christians to bring lost and hurting people into the fellowship of the church. Get them to church! – as if church is the thing that transforms peoples' lives. In my efforts to encourage people to learn how to share their faith, I often hear, "Bring people to church, that's great!" Sure, we need a vital ministry of inviting and bringing people to church.

What we cannot afford is a mentality that allows us to substitute an invitation to church for an invitation to Christ. Bringing a friend to church no more makes you a witness than taking your car to the garage makes you a mechanic. When Andrew met the Christ for the first time, he ran to find his brother Simon. When Andrew found Simon the Scriptures don't say, "And he brought him to church." It says "And he brought him to Jesus."

We all know this. And most of us would agree with the idea. Yet if you stop and think, when you're in someone's home, what do you talk about most – church or Christ? Evangelism is not inviting people to church.

Misconception #2. Evangelism is a concerted effort on the part of the church to show Christ to the world through consistent Christian living. When I invite people to learn how to share their faith I hear, "I witness through my life." Sure, we must witness through our lives. We must have a consistent walk that people can look to as an example. Jesus used life-style evangelism in reaching His disciples. They could see and observe Christ in every situation which arose. However, that was not the total scope of Christ's outreach. Neither should it be ours.

There are two major problems with being a witness through "living the life." First, the only people you can witness to are those who are very near you. That leaves out a lot of people God wants you to reach. The second problem with this kind of life-style evangelism is it doesn't bear witness to Christ. It bears witness to yourself. You're the one you witness for when you're witnessing by your life alone. When people can see your life without a verbal gospel testimony, their conclusion is, "John is a really great guy," or "Susan is one of the nicest gals I've ever met." That reflects well on you, or at the best on your church. The only problem is, *you* can't save their soul. They can't get to heaven because they know you. "Living the life" is not evangelism. Evangelism is turning peoples' eyes on Jesus Christ, not your good life.

Misconception #3. Evangelism is a gift from God to bring people into a saving relationship with Jesus Christ. Probably the most common response I hear in challenging people to evangelism is, "That's not my gift." I'm sorry. Evangelism is *not* a gift. If it is a gift as some understand it to be, most of us would be off the hook. Then evangelism would fall on the shoulders of only those few who have that spiritual gift.

Those who argue for evangelism as a spiritual gift use Ephesians 4:11 as their basis. But Paul is speaking here of *positions* held by gifted men, not gifts. And that's the only evidence anywhere that evangelism could by any stretch of the imagination be considered a spiritual gift.

I believe evangelism is a *responsibility* given to all Christians, and not a spiritual gift granted to a few. It is tied into a Christian's spiritual health, as much as prayer or Bible study. Both Christ's first and last commands given to His disciples dealt with evangelism. Jesus said, "Follow me and I will make you fishers of men" (Mark 1:17). Couldn't we conclude from this verse that if we are following Jesus we will be fishers of men? If we are not fishers of men, are we really followers of Jesus? "Go therefore and make disciples of all nations, baptizing them . . ." (Matthew 28:19-20). To whom did Jesus give this command? Just a few of His select disciples who had the spiritual gift of evangelism? No! He gave it to all of His disciples . . . on to all of us. Evangelism is not a spiritual gift – it is a *responsibility.*

The church today must align itself with the first century church in every way – worship, priorities, and unity. One of the dominant characteristics of the early church was its aggressive evangelism across the world. Not only the apostles, but every Christian was an evangelist! Acts 8:4 says, "Those (believers) who had been scattered preached the Word wherever they went."

The Christian's life is characterized by his fruit: love, joy, peace; his gifts: wisdom, discernment, healing; and his responsibilities: worship, prayer, Bible study, tithing. *Evangelism is a responsibility.* Would we say, "My gift is not tithing, it's prayer. I'll pray while others tithe." No! Tithing is a responsibility of the Christian's life. So is evangelism.

If evangelism is a responsibility, then we should give time and place to it. If it is an option or a gift, then we can do it "when we get an opportunity." But if it is a responsibility, then it deserves a time in our weekly schedule. We make a place for all our Christian responsibilities. We give time and place to worship. Christians give time and place to tithing. Christians give time and place to prayer and Bible study . . . if they don't, they notice spiritual decay in their lives. Why don't many Christians give time and place to evangelism? What if we took the same approach to worship as we do to evangelism? We would say, "Oh, I'll worship as I have the opportunities." How often would we worship? What if we said, "I'll read the Bible and pray as God prompts me to." How often would we read and pray? You see, for any responsibility in the Christian life we assign a time and a place. It doesn't mean we don't pray at other times or we don't worship at other times, but Sunday morning at 10:30 a.m. it means that we consider this Christian responsibility important enough to schedule a time and a place each week to do it.

Where has evangelism fit into your schedule? When was the time? Where was the place? For most Christians it is the ignored responsibility . . . it is done as opportunities "come and go." Taking this course will change all that. It will give evangelism time and place in your life for the next sixteen weeks. You will be obedient to what God has called all Christians to do.

For too long Christians have ignored the command of Christ to evangelize. We've let our light shine, but mostly we shine on each other – in the church where it's safe. My call to you is not to hide your light in prayer meeting or in Sunday school or worship services. Testimonies there are fine, but your light is not needed in the church. There's plenty of light under the bushel. A black and dying world needs that life-saving light . . . so come on out and shine . . . come on out from under the bushel!

LESSON 1

CONFESS AND REPENT

Men and women without Christ are the problem. Confession and repentance are the beginning of the answer. Often, when I begin to share my life in Christ with a prospect, Satan whispers in my ear, "He's heard this a million times. He knows exactly where you're coming from now. That's old hat!" That may be partly true. He probably has heard about Christ and many of the terms we use frequently in religious circles – "saved," "born again," "getting religion," or "being converted." We do live in a religiously saturated society.

However, it's a very rare person who knows the specific details of what is involved in obtaining eternal life in Christ if he isn't a Christian. A large part of Billy Graham's converts in his massive city-wide crusades are people who have attended church but have no assurance of eternal life. To hear about eternal life from time to time, and to understand the specifics of this experience are two different things!

Experiencing eternal life and forgiveness of sin begins with the realization that we have a need in the first place. This is where confession is so vitally important. It is difficult to search for an answer to a problem when a person hasn't even admitted his problem yet. This is why we turn to I John 1:9 as the first of four important and specific steps towards Christ.

> If we confess our sins, he is faithful and just and will forgive us our sins and purify us from all unrighteousness (1 John 1:9).

After reading this verse, point out that the key word is "confess." Ask the person what "confess" means to him. "What do we do when we confess something?" Asking that kind of question helps the conversation from being one-sided with you doing all the talking. No matter what kind of answer you receive, respond in a positive way . . . even if the answer surprises you. Clarify with a comment of your own. "Yes, that's right. When I think of confess, I think of admitting something or owning up to something I did or said. Does that make sense to you?" Always follow up your clarification with a question to see if the person is with you. Avoid phrases like, *"Now* do you understand?" Or, "Is it clear to you *now?" Whatever you say, don't preach down at them.* Stay on their level.

Once they've acknowledged they understand what confess means, make a simple application by saying, "In other words, to have eternal life, it's important to admit that we have a need of this eternal life. We have all fallen short." Again, ask if the person knows what you mean before going on by saying something like, "Does that make sense to you? Do you know what I mean? That really helped me when I first heard it." If there is confusion, then review. If not, move on to the next step with this transition statement, "That really helped me. And another verse that helped me was Acts 3:19."

This opens the door for a smooth transition to the next specific transition. Do not ask the person to take this step of confession yet. Wait until you share all four steps so that he can see the whole picture before committing himself.

Now that we have reached a point of confession, we are ready for the second important step toward Christ. To admit or confess is important, but there are many who admit their sins openly (some are even proud of their sins), but these in no way have eternal life. This is why repentance is so important. Repentance is not only admitting sin, but having deep sorrow for sin and a desire to turn away from it and go another direction.

> Repent, then, and turn to God, so that your sins may be wiped out, that times of refreshing may come from the Lord . . . (Acts 3:19).

This verse portrays the importance of repentance clearly. This verse is so good because it states the need for repentance in such a positive way. After reading the verse, point out that "repentance" is the key word. Ask the person what "repentance" means to him. Respond positively no matter what answer is given. Clarify his answer with your own understanding of the word repentance. Then see if he is with you in this understanding. "Yes, that's getting at what repentance means. When I think of repenting of something, I think of being sorry . . . so sorry I want to turn away from it, to make a change and not do it anymore. You know what I mean?" If he acknowledges, then move on. If not, review and clarify. Don't move too quickly or be in a hurry. Make sure he or she is with you.

Now, set up another smooth transition by making the statement, "That was an important verse in my life. I had to do something about my need, to turn around and head toward God."

There are two signs of an effective soul-winner: 1) He uses his ears as much as his mouth; and 2) He puts himself into the gospel plan. Putting your testimony and God's Word together is a powerful combination. Saying things like, "That was a very important verse in my life," does just that. It puts yourself into the salvation plan.

Set up the next verse by making this transition statement: "Let me share the third verse that has helped me." (The third verse is John 3:16, that you will study in Chapter 3.) Again, don't ask the person to repent yet. Wait until you share all four steps for eternal life.

The confess and repent section of the plan is the easiest to learn. This is why we begin learning the plan at this point. In order to solve any problem, a person has to admit he or she has a problem and wants to do something about it. If you get an evasive commitment it will probably be at this point – a prospect not truly admitting his need or wanting to change.

LESSON 1

HOMEWORK ASSIGNMENT

1. Contact both prayer partners. _____
2. Read Lesson 1 in its entirety. _____
3. Answer questions 1 through 10 in Lesson 1. _____
4. Memorize presentation outline in Lesson 1. _____
5. Practice the presentation at home. _____

QUESTIONS

1. What are the first two steps in the salvation plan?

2. To experience eternal life, you must begin with what step?

3. After we read 1 John 1:9 and point out the key word, what's the next thing to do?

4. What two things should you say to someone who has given you a wrong definition of "confess"?

5. What should you avoid saying at the end of an explanation of "confess"?

6. What is a good transition statement from "confess" to "repent"?

7. Why is Acts 3:19 a good verse on repentance?

8. Why isn't merely confessing our sin enough for God?

9. What are the two signs of an effective soul-winner?

10. Why are "confess" and "repent" so vital to a genuine commitment?

LESSON 1

PRESENTATION OUTLINE

II. Gospel
- **D. 1 John 1:9**
  - **1. What does confess mean to you?** ______
  - **2. To me confess means to admit.** ______
  - **3. To know we have eternal life, we must confess our need.** ______
  - **4. Does that make sense to you?** ______
- **E. Acts 3:19**
  - **1. What does repent mean to you?** ______
  - **2. To me repent means to be sorry.** ______
  - **3. To know we have eternal life, we must not only confess our need but be sorry enough to do something about that need.** ______
  - **4. Does that make sense to you?** ______

TRAINER'S USE ONLY:

Trainee's Name: ______________________________

Trainer's Name: ______________________________

Evaluation: ____Excellent ____Good ____Fair ____Poor

LESSON 2

MAN'S DILEMMA

When sharing Christ today, the biggest problem is not getting people saved, it's getting people lost! Because of a lack of emphasis on the need for salvation, there are many good, upstanding, moral, church-going people who simply aren't saved. These are hard to evangelize because they are not aware of their lost condition. It's difficult for them to see themselves as sinners because of their highly moral life-style.

For this reason, you should begin sharing the gospel plan with John 3:3 and Nicodemus.

> In reply Jesus declared, "I tell you the truth, no one can see the kingdom of God unless he is born again" (John 3:3).

Nicodemus is a good example of a very moral and religious man who didn't know how to have eternal life. First, point out *what Nicodemus did.* He came to Jesus after hearing Him teach and probably asked questions concerning the kingdom of God and eternal life. Then, point out *what Jesus said and didn't say.* He said, "You must be born again." Notice though what He didn't say. He didn't say anything about church attendance. He didn't say anything about helping the poor. He didn't say anything about being circumcised. He didn't say anything about just being good or trying to live uprightly. Finally, point out *who Nicodemus was.* Nicodemus was a Pharisee, a very religious man. He was not a heathen, not a wicked man, but a religious leader in his community. Yet Jesus said to this very religious and upright man, "You must be born again."

A good transition statement to the next verse is, "The reasons why Jesus said this to Nicodemus can be found in the next verse of Scripture, Romans 3:23.

> For all have sinned and fall short of the glory of God (Romans 3:23).

Point out that this verse includes yourself, your partner, your pastor, and religious leaders like Billy Graham, Mother Teresa, and the Pope. We've *all* sinned. We've all fallen short, including Nicodemus. Your strategy here is to put everyone in the boat before you put the person you're sharing with into the "sinners' boat." A good statement would be, "We've all sinned at some point. None of us can say that we're perfect, right?" By agreeing with your broad, all-inclusive statement, he puts himself into the boat too. Now that you have established the fact that all have sinned, you're ready for your next transition statement to Romans 6:23. The result of the sin that we all have is found in Romans 6:23.

> For the wages of sin is death, but the gift of God is eternal life in Christ Jesus our Lord (Romans 6:23).

This is your pivot verse. Up to Romans 6:23, you've been talking about man's problem. After Romans 6:23, you're going to spend the rest of the call with your prospect talking about God's answer. The problem is: all have sinned, and that means death. We deserve death; that's what a *wage* is, something we deserve. But (the pivot point) eternal life is a *gift* – something freely given out of love.

Your transition from Romans 6:23 sets up the next verse: "And it meant so much to me when I found out how I could receive this free gift. There are four verses of Scripture that tell us, specifically, how one can have eternal life." This sets up your transition to 1 John 1:9 (which you have already studied in the preceding chapter).

LESSON 2

HOMEWORK ASSIGNMENT

1. Contact both prayer partners. _____

2. Read Lesson 2 in its entirety. _____

3. Answer all the questions in Lesson 2. _____

4. Memorize presentation outline in Lesson 2. _____

5. Practice the presentation at home. _____

QUESTIONS

1. What is one of the biggest problems in sharing Christ today?

2. Why turn to John 3:3 first?

3. Why is Nicodemus a good example of someone who needed to be born again?

4. After you read John 3:3, what is the first thing you do? What is the second? What is the third?

5. What is a good transition statement from John 3:3 to Romans 3:23?

6. What five things do you say after reading Romans 3:23?

7. Why do you say these five things?

8. What is a good transition statement from Romans 3:23 to Romans 6:23?

9. There is something special about 6:23. What is it?

10. What are the two things being contrasted in Romans 6:23?

LESSON 2

PRESENTATION OUTLINE

Each chapter concludes with presentation outline as follows. The week's outline will always include everything you have studied so far in the course. The section of the presentation you are supposed to practice this week is in dark type for easy identification.

II. Gospel ______
- **A. John 3:3** ______
  1. **Who Nicodemus was** ______
  2. **What Nicodemus did** ______
  3. **What Jesus said and didn't say** ______
- **B. Romans 3:23** ______
  1. **Reasons for Jesus' answer found in this verse** ______
  2. **I have fallen short.** ______
  3. **My teammate has fallen short.** ______
  4. **Billy Graham, Mother Teresa, and the Pope have fallen short.** ______
  5. **We *all* have fallen short.** ______
- **C. Romans 6:23** ______
  1. **The result of our falling short – death** ______
  2. **The way out of that penalty – Jesus Christ** ______
- D. 1 John 1:9 ______
  1. What does "confess" mean to you? ______
  2. To me "confess" means to admit. ______
  3. To know we have eternal life, we must confess our need. ______
  4. Does that make sense to you? ______
- E. Acts 3:19 ______
  1. What does "repent" mean to you? ______
  2. To me "repent" means to be sorry. ______
  3. To know we have eternal life we must not only confess our need but be sorry enough to do something about that need. ______
  4. Does that make sense to you? ______

TRAINER'S USE ONLY:

Trainee's Name: ____________________________

Trainer's Name: ____________________________

Evaluation: ____Excellent ____Good ____Fair ____Poor

LESSON 3

BELIEVE AND RECEIVE

The first two scriptural steps to eternal life deal with what a person needs to do with *himself:* confess and repent. The last two steps deal with what he needs to do with *Jesus Christ:* to believe in Him and receive Him.

Before he can know for sure he has eternal life, he must come to grips with who Jesus Christ is. An ideal verse of Scripture to turn to is John 3:16.

> "For God so loved the world that He gave His one and only son, that whosoever believes in Him shall not perish, but have everlasting life" (John 3:16).

Point to "believe" as the key word in this verse. Share that some say Jesus was a good man or teacher but Jesus said, "I'm more than this . . . I'm the son of God who died on the cross for you." Most people have no trouble acknowledging Jesus Christ to be the Son of God. However, occasionally you'll meet someone who believes Jesus was merely a good man, but not God.

If this is the case, first ask yourself, does this person *want* to believe and is expressing honest doubt? Or, is he making the statement, "I will not believe"? This is important to discern. You can help the person in the first situation, but not in the second. The best direction to take in the second situation is to remain friendly, positive, and conclude the visit in the most gracious way possible. However, if the person wants to believe but can't because of honest doubt, point out that Jesus claimed to be the Son of God many times. He did it in front of the scribes and Pharisees, the common people of the countryside, and to His disciples. In fact, they crucified Jesus because He claimed to be the only Son of God.[1]

After establishing Christ's own claim to be God, point out that faith in Christ involves two things: 1) an *intellectual understanding* of Him; and, 2) an *experience* which comes as a result of encountering Christ in our lives. Then share the "Chair Illustration:"

> "We can examine a chair by studying it intellectually from all angles and be pretty confident that if we sat in it, it would hold us up. However, we cannot be 100 percent sure unless we give ourselves to the chair by sitting in it and lifting our feet off the ground. Only then can we have total confidence, because we've experienced the chair for ourselves. We can have that same confidence with Jesus Christ only when we give ourselves to Him totally and completely."

If the person you're sharing with does believe in Christ, then give a positive affirmation and set up a smooth transition by saying, "There is just one more scriptural step I want to share. It's the one that really opened the door for me in my own spiritual life."

Before going on, stop and give a short review of what you've covered up to this point. "In order to receive this gift of eternal life that we all need, we must first confess our need; second, repent – or be willing to do something about it; and third, believe Jesus Christ can meet our need." Then say, "There is just one more scriptural step we must take in order to know we have eternal life. It was this verse that really opened the door for me in my life. It is found in *John 1:12.*"

> Yet to all who received him, to those who believed in his name, he gave the right to become children of God (John 1:12).

As soon as you point out the key word – receive – and

[1]Matthew 16:15-17
John 11:25
Mark 14:61-62

have read the scripture, find a pen, pencil, Bible or any object readily available and share or adapt the "Pen Illustration:"

> "We're going to pretend that my partner here is in great financial need and that this pen I hold in my hand is pure gold." Tell the person you're sharing with how you've described the pen to your partner and you're freely giving the pen to him with no strings attached. Show how you're holding out the pen halfway between you and your partner. Then say, "Does he have the pen yet?" (Pause for answer: "No.") "What will he have to do to actually have this pen?" (Pause for answer: "Reach out and take it.") Then have your partner actually take the pen from your hand. Point out it's the same way with receiving Jesus Christ and eternal life; we must reach out and take Him into our lives.

A good transition statement to your next verse is: "Jesus gives us a promise in the last book of the Bible which is considered to be one of the greatest promises in all of Scripture. It's Revelation 3:20."

That transition statement sets up your commitment effort which you will study later in Chapter 5.

This week might be a good night to start actually sharing some of the plan you've been learning in the classroom and from reading this book. Once you begin to actually share part of this plan you'll begin to see God really using you in the lives of needy people. Then this course will really start coming alive, and you'll begin to see God use you in ways you never dreamed possible. Take the plunge!

LESSON 3

HOMEWORK ASSIGNMENT

1. Contact both prayer partners. _____

2. Read Lesson 3 in its entirety. _____

3. Answer questions at the end of Lesson 3. _____

4. Memorize presentation outline – Lesson 3. _____

5. Practice outline with a team member. _____

QUESTIONS

1. What do the first two scriptural steps to eternal life deal with?

2. What do the second two scriptural steps to eternal life deal with?

3. What verse is used to illustrate the importance of *"believe"*?

4. After reading this verse, what three things should you point out to the prospect according to the presentation outline?

5. If someone does not believe, what should you do?

6. According to the "Chair Illustration," what does faith in Christ involve?

7. You have just shared the step on "believe," and you are about to share the step on "receive." Just before you share "receive," what do you do?

8. What verse illustrates the need to *receive* Christ?

9. How do you illustrate the need to actually reach out and receive Christ?

10. After the illustration on "receive," what scripture do you turn to, and why?

LESSON 3

PRESENTATION OUTLINE

II. Gospel
- A. John 3:3 ______
  1. Who Nicodemus was ______
  2. What Nicodemus did ______
  3. What Jesus said and didn't say ______
- B. Romans 3:23 ______
  1. Reasons for Jesus' answer found in this verse ______ ______
  2. I have fallen short.
  3. My teammate has fallen short. ______
  4. Billy Graham, Mother Teresa, and the Pope have fallen short. ______ ______
  5. We *all* have fallen short. ______
- C. Romans 6:23
  1. The result of our falling short – death ______
  2. The way out of that penalty – Jesus Christ ______
- D. 1 John 1:9
  1. What does "confess" mean to you? ______
  2. To me "confess" means to admit. ______
  3. To know we have eternal life, we must confess our need. ______
  4. Does that make sense to you? ______
- E. Acts 3:19 ______
  1. What does "repent" mean to you? ______
  2. To me "repent" means to be sorry. ______
  3. To know we have eternal life we must not only confess our need but be sorry enough to do something about that need. ______
  4. Does that make sense to you? ______
- **F. John 3:16** ______
  1. **Key word – believe** ______
  2. **Some say Jesus is a good man or teacher.** ______
  3. **Jesus said He was the Son of God.** ______
  4. **Do you believe Jesus was the Son of God?** ______
- **G. John 1:12 and Revelation 3:20** ______
  1. **Review** ______
  2. **Most important step (John 1:12)** ______
  3. **The Receive Illustration** ______

TRAINER'S USE ONLY:

Trainee's Name: ______________________________

Trainer's Name: ______________________________

Evaluation: ____Excellent ____Good ____Fair ____Poor

LESSON 4

THE INTRODUCTION

The most strategic part of sharing your love for Christ with someone is the introduction. How you begin will play a big part in determining how you end up. It sets the tone for the rest of the calling experience.

The introduction is always marked as a time of nervousness and uncertainty – on your part as well as for the prospect. This nervousness tends to build until you've turned to the gospel plan.

The introduction has a threefold purpose. The first is to break the ice and put everyone at ease (except you). The second is to demonstrate to this person you are genuinely interested in him or her as a person. The third purpose is to assist you in directing the conversation smoothly and rapidly to the gospel plan. When I first began to share my faith, I went in fear and trembling. (I still do!) I'd be so nervous that I'd spend an hour just talking about anything that came to mind before I finally built up enough courage to pop the two questions. The result would be a long, drawn-out visit.

Personal background – As you begin your visit, take the *lead* in the conversation. Don't wait for the prospect to begin the conversation. Try to avoid long, awkward, silent periods when no one is talking. Begin asking about work, hobbies, and family. A good strategy at the outset of the conversation, even as you walk through the front door, is to look for items of interest around the house for which you can genuinely compliment them or talk about.

Look for obvious points of interest for them. You may

want to comment on their home, or ask how long they've lived there, ask about pictures, trophies, projects, pets, or anything that would indicate an interest in them as people. Always remember this person is an end – God's creation – not a means to an end. You're not there to boost your church's soul-winning program or your record of success or failure in soul-winning. You are there to share with someone Christ died for.

Church background – The next direction in your conversation is more toward their church background. The way to direct their conversation is simply to ask, "Is there a church you're attending now?" "How long have you attended that church?" If the person begins to share that he or she has been a faithful member of a certain church for twenty years, do not assume yet that he or she already knows Christ as a personal Savior. There are many "social Christians" today who have no idea at all what a personal relationship with Christ is. Or they know what it is, and yet have not experienced it.

If the person you're sharing with begins to raise doctrinal issues concerning the church, do not allow this to sidetrack you. It is next to impossible to disengage yourself from a doctrinal debate and get back to the gospel. Stay on track as best you can, yet be polite and cordial. Your business is to share your love for Christ, not argue or discuss theology.

Our church – The third step is to direct the conversation toward your church. Ask him or her how they happened to come to your church (if they are visitors). Ask them how they liked the service. Share a few aspects of the church that you appreciate or what your church means to you and your family. (In the case of a "cold turkey call," you could ask the person if they'd ever been to your church, or seen it or know anyone who attends there.)

The turning point – At this point you are ready to turn the conversation more directly to spiritual things. You have already led the conversation from the general family background to their church affiliation, so it will be no shock at all when you say, *"One of the reasons we've stopped by today is to find out how things are going spiritually. How are things going?"* Be up front and simple. They will respond with a variety of answers ranging from, "Things are okay," to "Never been worse," to "I have no idea." Respond to these by saying, "That's great," or "I appreciate your honesty or openness," or "I know what you mean, there've been times when I wasn't sure either." Then, follow this question by simply saying,

"There are a couple questions we have been asking folks pertaining to their spiritual life, and we were hoping we could ask them of you. Would that be okay?" Again, be up front and simple. If you are able to become confident in your plan, it will increase your effectiveness tremendously in helping someone find Christ.

Always remember, we don't want to cram Christ down anybody's throat, nor do we want to let one person get away without giving him or her a chance to receive Jesus Christ into their hearts. We must "earn" the right to ask these two important and personal questions by showing a caring and loving attitude. If we cannot show our love and concern for these people, then how can we share God's love for them?

THE TWO QUESTIONS

The mark of a good soul-winner is his or her ability to help people see themselves clearly in the light of God's eternity. In order to do this, a soul-winner must have a degree of courage and knowledge. He must be tactful, loving, and most of all have a real desire to see people saved. If a soul-winner really has a desire to see people find Christ, his fear and insecurity can be overcome.

To help someone reach a point of honest self-examination in the light of God's eternity is not an easy task. One reason it is so difficult is a person's natural desire to avoid facing failures and sins – even to himself, let alone in front of others. Thus, they will try to hide behind religious terms and clichés. Another reason is all the confusing terminology being used today. To be "born again" can mean a spiritual rebirth or a conservative issue in politics. To be "saved" can imply spiritual salvation or a religious fanatical group. To be a "Christian" can mean anything from having a personal relationship with Christ to simply being an American or Canadian.

The most strategic part of the plan is what the introduction has been leading up to, asking the person about his own relationship with Jesus Christ. The reason why this is such a strategic area is because it is very easy to give away the answer to the question.

For example, let's say I'm sharing with someone who I'm pretty sure needs Christ. However, he's hesitating to face his need. This is a natural feeling. He looks for a way to avoid the issue. (He may not even be aware that he is trying to avoid dealing with his sin.) So, when the question is asked, "Do you have a personal relationship with Jesus Christ?" his immediate response is, "Sure." Now, where do you go? You're pretty sure he needs salvation, but to go any further in the plan would be to virtually call him a liar. Or, if you said, "By the way, do you know that you're saved?" His response might be, "Yes, I'm saved." Where would you go from there?

When they say they are saved, do they mean what you mean? Are they talking about what you're talking about? Who knows? The best approach I've found is the use of two specifically worded questions.

Question 1: *Are you at a point in your spiritual life where you know for sure that you have eternal life?*

This question flows easily from your introductory question ("How are things going spiritually?") because you're using the same terms related to "spiritual life." Notice how all the confusing, double-meaning clichés are totally absent from this question. If the person you're sharing with answers, "No," or "I'm not sure," then he or she is a prime prospect for the gospel presentation. Whether they say yes, no, or "I hope so," always acknowledge their answer in a positive way. Always try to identify with him or her in their answer. Say something like, "That's great," or "I appreciate your honesty," or "I know what you mean, I've been there before myself."

Question 2: *If God were to ask why you should be allowed into His heaven, what reasons would you give?*

This question clearly uncovers what this person is putting his or her faith in. Nine times out of ten, you will get a "works" answer to that question. "I should be allowed in because I'm a good father," or "I'm a good housewife," or "I've been going to church all my life." When you get a response that relates to something other than receiving Christ as a personal Lord and Savior, then politely ask permission to share some verses of Scripture that have really helped you in your personal spiritual life.

On those very rare occasions when you do hear a right answer to those questions, have the person you are sharing with relate to you when and how he found Christ as his Lord and Savior. This gives him the chance to be a witness to you, and it gives you a chance to confirm in your own heart whether or not he really does know Christ. A genuine Christian should never resent the opportunity of telling the story of his salvation to another Christian brother or sister.

Because these questions are so important, they need to be memorized word for word. The biggest danger in any soul-winning call is the failure to really get to the issue at hand. Don't let your prospect off the hook too soon. Have enough courage to cut through all the cloudy terminology and get to the real issue. Does this person need Christ as Lord and Savior or not?

LESSON 4

HOMEWORK ASSIGNMENT

1. Contact both prayer partners. _____
2. Read Lesson 4 in your Student Workbook. _____
3. Answer all questions for Lesson 4. _____
4. Memorize Presentation Outline – Lesson 4. _____
5. Practice outline with a team member or family member. _____

QUESTIONS

1. What is the threefold purpose of the introduction?

2. What is the first thing you talk about as you begin your visit?

3. What should you avoid talking about?

4. What subjects are good to ask about at the start of your conversation?

5. What two things should you watch for when asking about their church background?

6. How do you turn the conversation from your church to the questions on eternal life?

7. What two reasons make it difficult for us to discover where someone is spiritually?

8. The two questions on eternal life are very strategic. Why?

9. What do you do after a prospect answers the first question?

10. The second question performs two functions. What are they?

LESSON 4

PRESENTATION OUTLINE

I. Introduction
- **A. Their Background**
  - **1. Work**
  - **2. Hobbies**
  - **3. Families**
- **B. Their Church**
  - **1. Where they attend**
  - **2. How long they have attended**
- **C. Our Church**
  - **1. How they happened to attend our church**
  - **2. Did they like the services**
  - **3. What the church has meant to me and my family**
- **D. Our Purpose**
  - **1. One of the reasons we stopped by is to find out how things are going with you spiritually. How are things going?**
  - **2. There are a couple of questions we have been asking folks pertaining to their spiritual life, and we were hoping we could ask them of you. Would that be okay?**
- **E. Two Questions**
  - **1. Are you at a point in your spiritual life where you know for sure you have eternal life?**
  - **2. If God were to ask why you should be allowed into heaven, what reasons would you give?**

II. The Gospel
- A. John 3:3
  - 1. Who Nicodemus was
  - 2. What Nicodemus did
  - 3. What Jesus said and didn't say
- B. Romans 3:23
  - 1. Reason for Jesus' answer found in this verse
  - 2. I have fallen short
  - 3. My teammate has fallen short
  - 4. Billy Graham, Mother Teresa, and the Pope have fallen short.
  - 5. We *all* have fallen short.
- C. Romans 6:23
  - 1. The result of our falling – death
  - 2. The way out of that penalty – Jesus Christ
- D. 1 John 1:9
  - 1. What does "confess" mean to you?
  - 2. To me "confess" means to admit.
  - 3. To know we have eternal life, we must confess our need.
  - 4. Does that make sense to you?
- E. Acts 3:19
  - 1. What does "repent" mean to you?
  - 2. To me "repent" means to be sorry.

3. To know we have eternal life, we must not only confess our need but be sorry enough to do something about our need. ______
4. Does that make sense to you? ______

F. John 3:16 – believe ______
1. Key word – believe ______
2. Some say Jesus is a good man or teacher. ______
3. Jesus was the Son of God. ______
4. Do you believe Jesus was the Son of God? ______

G. John 1:12 or Revelation 3:20 ______
1. Review ______
2. Most important step ______
3. The Receive Illustration ______

TRAINER'S USE ONLY:

Trainee's Name: ____________________________

Trainer's Name: ____________________________

Evaluation: ____Excellent ____Good ____Fair ____Poor

LESSON 5

THE COMMITMENT

You have successfully taken your prospect through the gospel plan. Now it's time to draw the net by asking him to open his heart to Jesus Christ.

You have just completed the "Pen Illustration" in the "Receive" step of John 1:12 by saying, "It's the same way with Jesus Christ. We reach out and take Him in." Now, set up Revelation 3:20 with a good transition statement. "Let me share with you what I consider to be one of the greatest promises in the Bible. Jesus is speaking here when He says in Revelation 3:20 these words . . .

> Here I am! I stand at the door and knock. If anyone hears my voice and opens the door, I will come in and eat with him, and he with me (Revelation 3:20).

After reading Revelation 3:20, take out a gospel tract and turn to the hearts diagram. A good introductory statement would be, "Let me show you a little diagram that really helped me see what Jesus is saying here."

Begin by explaining that the heart represents our life. The door represents the entry way to our life.

In the first heart, Christ is far from the scene and the door is closed tight. In the second heart, Christ is just outside the door knocking, asking to come in. The door is cracked a little as if the person is searching for some answers. In the third heart, the door is wide open and Christ has entered in, and a new relationship has begun.

Now ask the prospect which heart best represents his own life right now. If he points to the first or second heart, ask which heart he would like to have represent his life. If he answers the third kind of heart where Christ is in the door say, "This is how we go from one heart to the other. We go to God in prayer and simply take each one of those four steps I just shared with you." Give a very short example of the kind of prayer to be said.

> Lord Jesus, I confess my sins. I admit I have a spiritual need. And, Jesus, I repent of my sin. I want to turn and do something about my need. Lord Jesus, I believe You are the Son of God who died on the cross for me. I turn toward You as the only one who can meet my need. And Lord Jesus, right now I receive You by opening my life's door and inviting You in. In Jesus' name. Amen.

To quickly illustrate the kind of prayer ahead of time allows the prospect to know what he is going to say to God before he says it.

After the model prayer, ask the prospect, "Could you say this prayer tonight and really mean it?" If his response is yes, then tell him you will lead him through the prayer phrase by phrase. Then bow your head and begin to pray. As you pray, make sure your phrases are short enough for him to repeat without getting lost. (Be confident while drawing the net. The prospect needs to sense your calm assurance.)

At the close of the prayer, offer a word of prayer on your own for this new Christian. Let him hear you praying for his assurance. Let him hear you thanking God for him and his commitment.

If you don't feel comfortable using the tract at this point, an alternative is to use the picture illustration of Jesus knocking at a door. After reading Revelation 3:20, ask the prospect if he has ever seen the famous picture of Jesus knocking at the heart's door. (Small card pictures of this scene are available at most religious bookstores.) Ask the prospect if he has ever noticed the missing handle on the outside of that door. That's because the handle is only on the inside. Make the application by sharing, "The door represents the door to your heart or life. Jesus is knocking on that door asking to come in. Is there any good reason why you couldn't reach out and open that door and invite Christ into your life tonight?" Wording the question this way causes many people to realize there really isn't any good reason why they couldn't open that door. This then sets up your prayer time in the presentation method.

If he says no.

What do you do if the prospect says no to Christ? Don't give up! You don't know the reason behind the rejection. Always ask if there is some specific reason why he cannot take this last step. There could be some misunderstanding on his part as to the requirements or standards of becoming a Christian. Possibly the person believes he has to become better before asking Christ into his heart. If this is the case, there's no better time to discover and address the issue than now.

If he says, "Not yet."

In the event a person says he is simply not ready to take that last step, it's a good idea to find out why. At this point, it's up to the soul-winner's discretion as to how far to go. It is not difficult to discern his openness to the gospel if you're sensitive to the Spirit and use common sense. By this time in the presentation you can usually tell if a person has turned you off.

Keep in mind that the Holy Spirit is actively involved in your efforts and He will guide you in what to say and how often you should say it. We believe that God's divine appointment is working behind the scenes. Remember, many people you share with will never have as good an opportunity to accept Christ as you have just given them. So postponing such an important decision could be the same as rejecting Christ. Don't cram the gospel down their throats, yet don't be afraid to give them a clear-cut invitation.

If he says, "I've already done that."

Go back to the second question (why God should allow him into heaven) and explain why you shared these scriptures. Remind him of the answer he gave and how that indicated to you what he's putting his faith in today. Affirm his prior commitment and ask if he would like to make a re-commitment or rededicate himself to that relationship . . . to put his faith in Jesus alone.

LESSON 5

HOMEWORK ASSIGNMENT

1. Contact both prayer partners. _____

2. Read Lesson 5 in your student workbook. _____

3. Answer all questions for Lesson 5. _____

4. Memorize Presentation Outline – Lesson 5. _____

5. Practice outline with team member or family member. _____

QUESTIONS

1. What verse do we use to begin "drawing the net"?

2. What transition statement do we use to set up this verse?

3. What's the first thing we do after reading Revelation 3:20?

4. After you take out your gospel tract what is a good introductory sentence to lead into the heart diagram?

5. After explaining the heart diagram to a prospect, what is the first question you ask him? What is the second question you ask him?

6. A prospect has just pointed to the last heart indicating that's where he wants his life to be. What four things do you do before you lead that prospect in the sinner's prayer?

7. What do you do if the prospect says no to your invitation to Jesus Christ?

8. What do you do if a prospect says he is not ready to open his life to Christ?

9. What is an alternative way to "draw the net" without using the tract?

10. What do you do if a person says he has already done that?

LESSON 5

PRESENTATION OUTLINE

I. Introduction
   A. Their Background
      1. Work
      2. Hobbies
      3. Families
   B. Their Church
      1. Where they attend
      2. How long they have attended
   C. Our Church
      1. How they happened to attend our church
      2. Did they like the services
      3. What the church has meant to me and my family
   D. Our Purpose
      1. One of the reasons we stopped by is to find out how things are going with you spiritually. How are things going?
      2. There are a couple of questions we have been asking folks pertaining to their spiritual life, and we were hoping we could ask them of you. Would that be okay?
   E. Two Questions
      1. Are you at a point in your spiritual life where you know for sure you have eternal life?
      2. If God were to ask why you should be allowed into heaven, what reasons would you give?

II. Gospel
   A. John 3:3
      1. Who Nicodemus was
      2. What Nicodemus did
      3. What Jesus said and didn't say
   B. Romans 3:23
      1. Reasons for Jesus' answer found in this verse
      2. I have fallen short
      3. My teammate has fallen short
      4. Billy Graham, Mother Teresa, and the Pope have fallen short.
      5. We *all* have fallen short.
   C. Romans 6:23
      1. The result of our falling short – death
      2. The way out of that penalty – Jesus Christ
   D. 1 John 1:9
      1. What does "confess" mean to you?
      2. To me "confess" means to admit.
      3. To know we have eternal life, we must confess our need.
      4. Does that make sense to you?
   E. Acts 3:19
      1. What does "repent" mean to you?
      2. To me "repent" means to be sorry.
      3. To know we have eternal life, we must not only confess our need but be sorry enough to do something about our need.
      4. Does that make sense to you?

F. John 3:16 – believe
   1. Key word – believe
   2. Some say Jesus is a good man or teacher.
   3. Jesus said He was the Son of God.
   4. Do you believe Jesus was the Son of God?

G. John 1:12 and Revelation 3:20
   1. Review
   2. Most important step (John 1:12)
   3. The Receive Illustration

III. Commitment
   A. Revelation 3:20 – God's promise to come in
   B. Tract – heart diagram
   C. "Which best represents your life?/Which would you like to represent your life?"

   OPTION:
   a. Revelation 3:20 – God's promise to come in
   b. Picture: Jesus at heart's door
   c. "Is there any good reason why you couldn't take that last step tonight?"

   D. Prayer Instruction
      1. The way we open our heart to Christ is through prayer
      2. Prayer example
      3. Can you pray this and mean it?
   E. Short, simple prayer repeating after you
      1. Short phrases
      2. Go through four steps
      3. Pray for new Christian's assurance

TRAINER'S USE ONLY:

Trainee's Name: ____________________

Trainer's Name: ____________________

Evaluation: ___Excellent ___Good ___Fair ___Poor

LESSON 6

IMMEDIATE FOLLOW-UP

After you have successfully led the new believer to Christ, immediate follow-up must take place to give the new believer a chance to grow and mature. Immediate follow-up occurs after the commitment, but before you leave the house.

First, after your prayer, make sure the new believer knows how thrilled you are about his decision for Christ. Make him aware of the important significance this commitment has on his life. This is his spiritual birthday! It's important here to be yourself. Don't express your joy in an unnatural way. Usually reaching out and shaking his hand, or patting or squeezing his arm is an effective way to warmly express your happiness. Say something like, "I'm so thrilled about the decision you just made." Or, "I believe you've just made the most important decision in your life."

Next, take your gospel tract and write on the back "1 John 5:11-15." One of the most common struggles a new believer has is doubt. He says to himself, "Did anything really happen to me?" Ask the new believer to read these verses three times before going to bed that night.

Then turn to the back page of the tract and ask, "Where do you go from here?" Run through each of the four suggestions commenting briefly on each.

1. *"Prayer* is our way of talking to God."
2. *"The Bible* is God's way of talking to us."
3. *"Church* is our way to worship and fellowship with God and other believers."

4. *"Telling a friend* encourages someone else, and helps establish your own faith."

Ask the new believer if he can think of one good friend from the past. Ask what would happen if suddenly that friend moved 2,000 miles away. "Let's say you never called each other. You never wrote each other. You never visited each other . . . for thirty years. What would happen to that relationship?" Let him answer. (It would fade away.) "The same is true in your new relationship with Jesus Christ." Be up front at this point. Tell the new believer, "If this commitment is just a passing fancy, what's happened tonight won't have much impact on your life. You've got to nurture this relationship just like any other."

Share with this new believer, "We would like to help you at this point. We feel a sense of responsibility to all those we bring to Christ. We don't want to come in here, lead you to Christ, and then just abandon you. We care about you too much for that." Now share how you can help.

New Life Class. First, talk about the New Life Class if your church has one started. Tell them, "It's just for new believers, and everybody will be a new Christian just like you are." Ask if you can pick him up and take him. If he already has a church, ask if he would be open to a discipler (someone from your church who would stop by his home at least once a week for prayer, Bible study, encouragement, and moral support).

Twenty-four-Hour Call-Back. Ask if you could stop back tomorrow for only five minutes or so, just to drop off some helpful material.

Public Commitment. Finally say, "One last thing that I would really recommend is a public commitment. The one thing that really helped me more than anything else was when I put my faith in Christ, I stood up to say so by going to the altar and praying at the close of the service. It was scary, but I felt great after I did it. It really cements your commitment in your heart by going forward. There will be opportunity Sunday morning at the end of the service if you want to do this. You could meet our pastor then, too. So keep it in mind. If you do go, I'll go with you."

Address and Phone. Finally, before you leave, check to make sure you have his right name, address, and phone number. If you wish, you could close with a final prayer. As you exit, say as a final word, "See you tomorrow," at the specific time you arranged for the twenty-four-hour call-back.

LESSON 6

HOMEWORK ASSIGNMENT

1. Contact both prayer partners. _____

2. Read Lesson 6 in its entirety. _____

3. Answer questions 1 through 10 in Lesson 6. _____

4. Memorize Presentation Outline in Lesson 6. _____

5. Practice outline with team members. _____

QUESTIONS

1. When does immediate follow-up take place?

2. What do you do immediately after you've led your prospect through the sinner's prayer?

3. What's the most common problem of new believers?

4. What verse is good to deal with this problem?

5. What four things are essential to a new believer's spiritual development?

6. How can you illustrate the importance of nurturing a relationship with Jesus Christ to keep it from fading away?

7. What's something we as a church can do to help a new believer grow?

8. If a new believer is already actively involved in another church, what option of follow-up is available?

9. What verse of Scripture supports the importance of a public commitment?

10. Just before you leave the house, what should you check on with the new believer?

LESSON 6

PRESENTATION OUTLINE

I. Introduction
   A. Their Background
      1. Work
      2. Hobbies
      3. Families
   B. Their Church
      1. Where they attend
      2. How long they have attended
   C. Our Church
      1. How they happened to attend our church
      2. Did they like the services
      3. What the church has meant to me and my family
   D. Our Purpose
      1. One of the reasons we stopped by is to find out how things are going with you spiritually. How are things going?
      2. There are a couple of questions we have been asking folks pertaining to their spiritual life, and we were hoping we could ask them of you. Would that be okay?
   E. Two Questions
      1. Are you at a point in your spiritual life where you know for sure you have eternal life?
      2. If God were to ask why you should be allowed into heaven, what reasons would you give?

II. The Gospel
   A. John 3:3
      1. Who Nicodemus was
      2. What Nicodemus did
      3. What Jesus said and didn't say
   B. Romans 3:23
      1. Reason for Jesus' answer found in this verse
      2. I have fallen short
      3. My teammate has fallen short
      4. Billy Graham, Mother Teresa, and the Pope have fallen short.
      5. We *all* have fallen short.
   C. Romans 6:23
      1. The result of our falling – death
      2. The way out of that penalty – Jesus Christ
   D. I John 1:9
      1. What does "confess" mean to you?
      2. To me "confess" means to admit.
      3. To know we have eternal life, we must confess our need.
      4. Does that make sense to you?
   E. Acts 3:19
      1. What does "repent" mean to you?
      2. To me "repent" means to be sorry.
      3. To know we have eternal life, we must not only confess our need but be sorry enough to do something about our need.
      4. Does that make sense to you?

F. John 3:16 – believe ________
1. Key word – believe ________
2. Some say Jesus is a good man or teacher. ________
3. Jesus was the Son of God. ________
4. Do you believe Jesus was the Son of God? ________

G. John 1:12 ________
1. Review ________
2. Most important step ________
3. The Receive Illustration ________

III. Commitment ________
A. Revelation 3:20 – God's promise to come in. ________
B. Tract – heart diagram ________
C. "Which best represents your life?/Which would you like to represent your life?" ________

OPTION:
a. Revelation 3:20 – God's promise to come in ________
b. Picture: Jesus at heart's door ________
c. "Is there any good reason why you couldn't take that last step tonight?" ________

D. Prayer Instruction ________
1. The way we open our heart to Christ is through prayer. ________
2. Prayer example. ________
3. Can you pray this and mean it? ________

E. Short, simple prayer repeating after you. ________
1. Short phrases. ________
2. Go through four steps. ________
3. Pray for new Christian's assurance. ________

IV. Immediate Follow-up ________
A. Congratulations ________
B. Gospel tract ________
1. Write assurance verse ________
2. Turn to last page
C. Building relationship with Christ ________
1. Compare with childhood friend ________
2. This is how we can help ________
a. New Life Class (option: discipler) ________
b. Twenty-four-hour call-back – study material ________
c. Witnessing – public commitment ________
D. Name, address, phone ________

TRAINER'S USE ONLY:

Trainee's Name: ______________________________

Trainer's Name: ______________________________

Evaluation: ____Excellent ____Good ____Fair ____Poor

LESSON 7

EXTENDED FOLLOW-UP

The critical week of the new believer's life in Jesus Christ is the first week of life. Just as a newborn baby is watched over carefully the first days of life, so a newly born believer needs careful attention the first days of his new life in Christ. The following schedule is based on a Thursday calling night. Of course it can be adapted for any calling night.

Thursday – The extended follow-up begins the minute the team gets back to the church for share and prayer time. Three things need to happen before the team goes home:

1. *Personal Letter.* Every team member sits down and writes a personal letter to the new believer to be mailed by the church throughout the week.

2. *Assignments.* The pastor makes sure all members of the soul-winning team know their specific assignments to be carried out for the next seven days. Each team member will play a part.

3. *Prayer partners.* Contact is made with the team's prayer partners so that prayer support begins to rise up all over the city for this new believer and the follow-up process.

Friday – The next night, trainee #1 (whichever of the two trainees on the team who had the most in common with the new believer) makes the twenty-four-hour call-back to drop off valuable follow-up material (a book of salvation, small booklets). The trainee should express his appreciation for the previous night's visit and briefly explain the material. The trainee should remind the new believer of next week's "seven-day call-back" and mention seeing him or her this Sunday morning when they are picked up for New Life Sunday School Class at church.

Saturday – On the second night after the soul-winning call, the trainer calls on the telephone to see how things are going and to invite the new believer to a meal after church on Sunday morning. Conclude the call with a brief prayer of support for the new believer. On the third night after the soul-winning call, the first personal letter arrives in the mail (mailed the day before) written by trainee #2. This note reminds the new believer of the next day's activities and how much the team is looking forward to seeing him or her on Sunday morning.

Sunday – Trainee #1 picks up the new believer for Sunday school. The rest of the team greets him or her at the church door. Then the new believer is taken to New Life Class and introduced to the teacher, the host, and hostess. If your church has a discipleship program, a discipler should also be there to meet the new believer and follow up in the weeks ahead. If not, a discipler needs to go with the soul-winning team to meet the new believer for the first time during the seven-day call-back. If a public commitment is made, the team should accompany the new believer to the altar. After church, the new believer is taken for fellowship by the soul-winner to the prearranged meal.

Monday – On the following day, the second personal letter arrives with an encouraging word.

Tuesday – Trainee #2 calls on the telephone to say how good it was to have the new believer in church Sunday and reminds the new convert of the seven-day call-back on Thursday.

Wednesday – The third personal letter (from the trainer this time) arrives, saying he is looking forward to seeing the new convert on Thursday night (the seven-day call-back).

Thursday – Finally, on the seven-day call-back, the team stops by the new believer's home again. Three things should happen during this call-back. First, *how did last week go?* If he came to church Sunday, how did he like it? If he failed to come, why? Could he come this Sunday?

Second, *are there any questions?* Are there any doubts in his mind? Is he asking, "Did I really get it?" Review the salvation plan briefly, emphasizing God's promise in Revelation 3:20, and 1 John 5:11-15, we can *know.*

Third, what's ahead? Don't leave the believer's home without something for him to look forward to. Does he have a discipleship meeting lined up? Is he planning on New Life Class this Sunday? Always give him something to look forward to where he knows he will be touched by a loving and caring church community.

LESSON 7

HOMEWORK ASSIGNMENT

1. Contact both prayer partners. _____
2. Read Lesson 7 in its entirety. _____
3. Answer questions 1 through 5 in Lesson 7. _____
4. Memorize Presentation Outline in Lesson 7. _____
5. Practice outline with team member. _____

QUESTIONS

1. When does extended follow-up begin?

2. What three things need to happen before the team goes home?

3. What should happen on the first Sunday following a commitment?

4. What should be discussed and touched upon during the seven-day call-back?

5. In the following space, using your soul-winning night, outline what things should happen each day during the first week of a new believer's life.

LESSON 7

PRESENTATION OUTLINE

I. Introduction ____
   A. Their Background ____
      1. Work ____
      2. Hobbies ____
      3. Families ____
   B. Their Church ____
      1. Where they attend ____
      2. How long they have attended ____
   C. Our Church ____
      1. How they happened to attend our church ____
      2. Did they like the services ____
      3. What the church has meant to me and my family ____
   D. Our Purpose ____
      1. One of the reasons we stopped by is to find out how things are going with you spiritually. How are things going? ____
      2. There are a couple of questions we have been asking folks pertaining to their spiritual life, and we were hoping we could ask them of you. Would that be okay? ____
   E. Two Questions ____
      1. Are you at a point in your spiritual life where you know for sure you have eternal life? ____
      2. If God were to ask why you should be allowed into heaven, what reasons would you give? ____

II. The Gospel ____
   A. John 3:3 ____
      1. Who Nicodemus was ____
      2. What Nicodemus did ____
      3. What Jesus said and didn't say ____
   B. Romans 3:23 ____
      1. Reason for Jesus' answer found in this verse ____
      2. I have fallen short ____
      3. My teammate has fallen short ____
      4. Billy Graham, Mother Teresa, and the Pope have fallen short. ____
      5. We *all* have fallen short. ____
   C. Romans 6:23 ____
      1. The result of our falling – death ____
      2. The way out of that penalty – Jesus Christ ____
   D. 1 John 1:9 ____
      1. What does "confess" mean to you? ____
      2. To me "confess" means to admit. ____
      3. To know we have eternal life, we must confess our need. ____
      4. Does that make sense to you? ____
   E. Acts 3:19 ____
      1. What does "repent" mean to you? ____
      2. To me "repent" means to be sorry. ____
      3. To know we have eternal life, we must not only confess our need but be sorry enough to do something about our need. ____
      4. Does that make sense to you? ____

F. John 3:16 – believe
   1. Key word – believe
   2. Some say Jesus is a good man or teacher.
   3. Jesus was the Son of God.
   4. Do you believe Jesus was the Son of God?
G. John 1:12
   1. Review
   2. Most important step
   3. The Receive Illustration

III. Commitment
   A. Revelation 3:20 – God's promise to come in
   B. Tract – Heart diagram
   C. "Which best represents your life?/Which would you like to represent your life?"

   OPTION:

   a. Revelation 3:20 – God's promise to come in.
   b. Picture: Jesus at heart's door.
   c. "Is there any good reason why you couldn't take that last step tonight?"

   D. Prayer Instruction.
      1. The way we open our heart to Christ is through prayer.
      2. Prayer example.
      3. Can you pray this and mean it?
   E. Short, simple prayer repeating after you.
      1. Short phrases.
      2. Go through four steps.
      3. Pray for new Christian's assurance.

IV. Immediate Follow-up
   A. Congratulations
   B. Gospel tract
      1. Write assurance verse
      2. Turn to last page
   C. Building relationship with Christ
      1. Compare with childhood friend
      2. This is how we can help
         a. New Life Class (option: discipler)
         b. Twenty-four-hour call-back – study material
         c. Witnessing – public commitment
   D. Name, address, phone

V. Extended Follow-up
   A. First night – commitment night
      1. All prayer-grams prepared
      2. All follow-up assignments made
      3. All prayer partners notified
   B. Second night – twenty-four-hour call-back
      1. Trainee #1 delivers and goes over material
      2. Reaffirms Sunday morning appointment for New Life Class
      3. Reminder of seven-day call-back
   C. Third night
      1. Trainer checks up on new believer by phone
      2. Invitation to Sunday noon meal
      3. Pray over phone for new believer

D. Fourth night ______
   1. Letter arrives from trainee #2 ______
   2. Reminder in the letter of New Life Class on Sunday ______
E. Fifth day ______
   1. Trainee #1 picks up new believer ______
   2. Team greets new believer at door ______
   3. Team accompanies new believer to New Life Class ______
   4. New believer is introduced to pastor, host, discipler ______
   5. Possible public commitment made ______
   6. Meal with new believer ______
   7. Reminder of seven-day call-back ______
F. Sixth night ______
   1. Trainee #2 makes phone call ______
   2. Letter arrives from trainee #1 ______
G. Tuesday – seventh night ______
   1. Prayer-gram arrives from trainer ______
   2. Looking forward to tomorrow's visit ______
H. Eighth night – Seven-day call-back ______
   1. How did last week go ______
   2. Are there any questions? ______
   3. What's ahead? ______

TRAINER'S USE ONLY:

Trainee's Name: ______________________________

Trainer's Name: ______________________________

Evaluation: ____Excellent ____Good ____Fair ____Poor

CONCLUSION

Now you're ready. You're prepared. You know what to say and how to say it. You know how to build rapport. You know how to find out where someone is in their spiritual life and to take them into the Bible. You know how to draw the net. You've learned to follow up their decisions for Christ.

Now pick up the ball and run. Use it or lose it. The best way to sharpen your skills is using them in the field. Your confidence will grow with every visit you make. Continue to practice putting yourself into the plan. Use your ears as much as your mouth. God's Word and your own experience are a powerful combination.

Learn quickly to rejoice and feel part of another team's success. If the only time you're excited is when your team has victories, you will have a long, disappointing semester. If you lead someone to Christ three times out of sixteen you've had tremendous success. So rejoice in the victories of other teams.

Keep in mind, *you* can't save anyone . . . that's Christ's job. The only thing you have control over is your faithful witness. Learn quickly what real success is. Real success is simply sharing Jesus. When the twelve excitedly returned from being sent out, what did Jesus say? "Do not rejoice over the fact the demons submitted or that people were healed. Rejoice that your name is written down, that you have been obedient."

Begin to develop a personal prospect list: golf partners, family members you've never shared with, neighbors you've talked with over the fence. Keep a list of fringe people who come and go from the church. Don't skip over your "Jerusalems"; they are your hottest prospects.

After five or six weeks, take a break from your weekly schedule. Even Jesus took retreat times. You don't want to burn out in this ministry. Just remember, in your retreat, don't climb back under the bushel! It took too much to get you out from under there in the first place. Never again become satisfied with life under the bushel.

Finally, when your break is over, and it's time to re-enter the harvest field, don't go alone. Help someone else take the route you just took. Someone invested in you to get you out from under the bushel; now invest yourself in someone else. You'll learn things training others that you never could have learned while being trained. Winning a soul to Christ is addition. Training a soul-winner is multiplication. Stay out from under the bushel and keep multiplying!

Diary of a Soul-Winner

Week 1

Diary of a Soul-Winner

Week 2

Diary of a Soul-Winner

Week 3

Diary of a Soul-Winner

Week 4

Diary of a Soul-Winner

Week 5

Diary of a Soul-Winner

Week 6

Diary of a Soul-Winner

Week 7

Diary of a Soul-Winner

Week 8

Diary of a Soul-Winner

Week 9

Diary of a Soul-Winner

Week 10

Diary of a Soul-Winner

Week 11

Diary of a Soul-Winner

Week 12

Diary of a Soul-Winner

Week 13

Diary of a Soul-Winner

Week 14

Diary of a Soul-Winner

Week 15

Diary of a Soul-Winner

Week 16